OUT AND ABOUT

OUT AND ABOUT
Poems of the Outdoors

Chosen by Raymond Wilson

Illustrated by Mike Daley

VIKING KESTREL

VIKING KESTREL

Penguin Books Ltd, Harmondsworth, Middlesex, England
Viking Penguin Inc., 40 West 23rd Street, New York, New York 10010, U.S.A.
Penguin Books Australia Ltd, Ringwood, Victoria, Australia
Penguin Books Canada Ltd, 2801 John Street, Markham, Ontario, Canada L3R 1B4
Penguin Books (N.Z.) Ltd, 182–190 Wairau Road, Auckland 10, New Zealand

First published 1987

Printed in Great Britain by
Butler & Tanner Ltd, Frome & London
Filmset in Monophoto Baskerville

British Library Cataloguing in Publication Data

Out and about : poems of the outdoors.
  1. Outdoor life——Poetry 2. English poetry
I. Wilson, Raymond, *1925–*
821'.008'036   PR1195.08

  ISBN 0–670–81714–7

Contents

Come! Come Away!

Highways and Byways

Fairs, Sports and Games

The Country Life

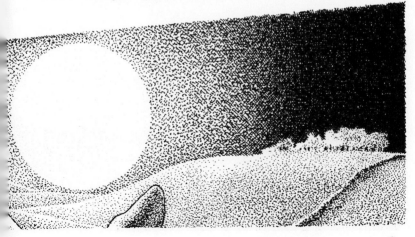

Vagabonds and Wanderers

Adventure

Journey's End

Index and Acknowledgements

Come! Come Away!

Tony O

Over the bleak and barren snow
A voice there came a-calling;
'Where are you going to, Tony O!
Where are you going this morning?'

'I am going where there are rivers of wine,
The mountains bread and honey;
There Kings and Queens do mind the swine,
And the poor have all the money.'

Unknown

When Green Buds Hang

When green buds hang in the elm like dust
    And sprinkle the lime like rain,
Forth I wander, forth I must,
    And drink of life again.
Forth I must by hedgerow bowers
    To look at the leaves uncurled,
And stand in the fields where cuckoo-flowers
    Are lying about the world.

A. E. Housman

Amid the Flying Clouds . . .

Amid the flying clouds the blue sky dreams;
The earth is trembling at the approach of Spring,
And, lashed by heavy showers, the cool air seems
As though upon some quest 'twere hurrying.

A sudden longing brings a stab of pain,
So hard it grips your heart on such a day:
You'd like to jump on board the fastest train
That thunders down from Rome to Naples Bay.

J. S. Machar
**translated from the Czech by
E. Osers and J. K. Montgomery**

18

Poetry of Departure

Sometimes you hear, fifth-hand,
As epitaph:
*He chucked up everything
And just cleared off,*
And always the voice will sound
Certain you approve
This audacious, purifying,
Elemental move.

And they are right, I think.
We all hate home
And having to be there:
I detest my room,
Its specially-chosen junk,
The good books, the good bed,
And my life, in perfect order:
So to hear it said

He walked out on the whole crowd
Leaves me flushed and stirred,
Like *Then she undid her dress*
Or *Take that you bastard*;
Surely I can, if he did?
And that helps me stay
Sober and industrious.
But I'd go today,

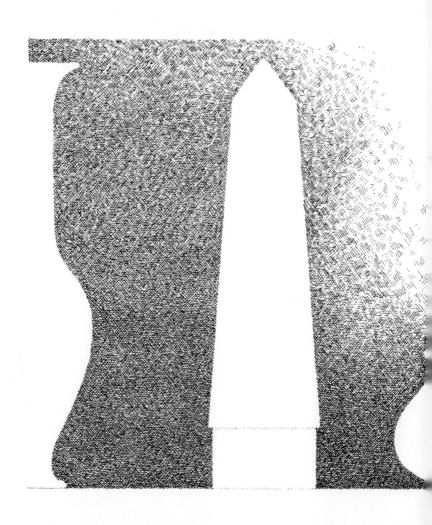

20

Yes, swagger the nut-strewn roads,
Crouch in the fo'c'sle
Stubbly with goodness, if
It weren't so artificial,
Such a deliberate step backwards
To create an object:
Books; china; a life
Reprehensibly perfect.

Philip Larkin

My Heart's in the Highlands

My heart's in the Highlands, my heart is not here;
My heart's in the Highlands a-chasing the deer;
Chasing the wild deer, and following the roe,
My heart's in the Highlands, wherever I go.
Farewell to the Highlands, farewell to the North,
The birthplace of valour, the country of worth;
Wherever I wander, wherever I rove,
The hills of the Highlands for ever I love.

Farewell to the mountains, high covered with snow;
Farewell to the straths and green valleys below;
Farewell to the forests and wild-hanging woods;
Farewell to the torrents and loud-pouring floods.
My heart's in the Highlands, my heart is not here;
My heart's in the Highlands, a-chasing the deer;
Chasing the wild deer, and following the roe,
My heart's in the Highlands, wherever I go.

Robert Burns

The Lake Isle of Innisfree

I will arise and go now, and go to Innisfree,
And a small cabin build there,
　　　　of clay and wattles made:
Nine bean-rows will I have there,
　　　　a hive for the honey-bee,
And live alone in the bee-loud glade.

And I shall have some peace there,
　　　　for peace comes dropping slow,
Dropping from the veils of the morning
　　　　to where the cricket sings:
There midnight's all a glimmer,
　　　　and noon a purple glow,
And evening full of the linnet's wings.

I will arise and go now,
　　　　for always night and day
I hear lake water lapping
　　　　with low sounds by the shore;
While I stand on the roadway,
　　　　or on the pavements grey,
I hear it in the deep heart's core.

W. B. Yeats

A Boy's Song

Where the pools are bright and deep,
Where the grey trout lies asleep,
Up the river and over the lea,
That's the way for Billy and me.

Where the blackbird sings the latest,
Where the hawthorn blooms the sweetest,
Where the nestlings chirp and flee,
That's the way for Billy and me.

Where the mowers mow the cleanest,
Where the hay lies thick and greenest,
There to track the homeward bee,
That's the way for Billy and me.

Where the hazel bank is steepest,
Where the shadow falls the deepest,
Where the clustering nuts fall free,
That's the way for Billy and me.

This I know, I love to play,
Through the meadow, among the hay,
Up the water and over the lea,
That's the way for Billy and me.

James Hogg

A Great Time

Sweet Chance, that led my steps abroad,
　　Beyond the town, where wild flowers grow –
A rainbow and a cuckoo, Lord,
　　How rich and great the times are now!
　　　　Know, all ye sheep
　　　　And cows, that keep
On staring that I stand so long
　　In grass that's wet from heavy rain –
A rainbow and a cuckoo's song
　　May never come together again;
　　　　May never come
　　　　This side the tomb.

W. H. Davies

Where the Pelican Builds

The horses were ready, the rails were down,
　　But the riders lingered still –
One had a parting word to say
　　And one had his pipe to fill.
Then they mounted, one with granted prayer,
　　And one with grief unguessed.
'We are going,' they said, as they rode away,
　　'Where the pelican builds her nest!'

They had told us of pastures wide and green,
　　To be sought past the sunset's glow;
Of rifts in the ranges, opal-lit,
　　And gold 'neath the river's flow.
And thirst and hunger were banished words,
　　When they spoke of that unknown West;
No drought they dreaded, no flood they feared
　　Where the pelican builds her nest.

The creek at the ford was but fetlock deep,
　　When we watched them crossing there;
The rains have replenished it thrice since then,
　　And thrice has the rock lain bare.
But the waters of Hope have flowed and fled,
　　And never from blue hill's breast,
Come back – by the sun and the sands devoured –
　　Where the pelican builds her nest.

Mary Hannay Foott

A Wanderer's Song

A wind's in the heart of me, a fire's in my heels,
I am tired of brick and stone and rumbling
  wagon-wheels;
I hunger for the sea's edge, the limits of the land,
Where the wild old Atlantic is shouting on the sand.

Oh I'll be going, leaving the noises of the street,
To where a lifting foresail-foot is yanking at the sheet;
To a windy, tossing anchorage where yawls and ketches
  ride,
Oh I'll be going, going, until I meet the tide.

And first I'll hear the sea-wind, the mewing of the gulls,
The clucking, sucking of the sea about the rusty hulls,
The songs at the capstan in the hooker warping out,
And then the heart of me'll know I'm there or
  thereabout.

Oh I am tired of brick and stone, the heart of me is sick,
For windy green, unquiet sea, the realm of Moby Dick;
And I'll be going, going, from the roaring of the wheels,
For a wind's in the heart of me, a fire's in my heels.

John Masefield

O To Sail

O to sail in a ship,
To leave this steady unendurable land,
To leave the tiresome sameness of the streets, the
    sidewalks and the houses,
To leave you, O you solid motionless land,
    and entering a ship,
To sail and sail and sail!

Walt Whitman

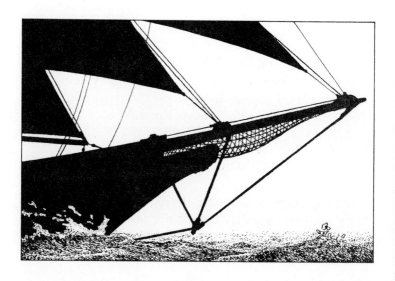

The Sailor Boy

He rose at dawn and, fired with hope,
  Shot o'er the seething harbour-bar,
And reach'd the ship and caught the rope,
  And whistled to the morning star.

And while he whistled long and loud
  He heard a fierce mermaiden cry;
'O boy, tho' thou art young and proud,
  I see the place where thou wilt lie.

'The sands and yeasty surges mix
  In caves about the dreary bay,
And on thy ribs the limpet sticks,
  And in thy heart the scrawl shall play.'

scray — Common Tern, Sea Swallow

'Fool,' he answer'd, 'death is sure
  To those that stay and those that roam,
But I will nevermore endure
  To sit with empty hands at home.

'My mother clings about my neck,
  My sisters crying, "Stay for shame;"
My father raves of death and wreck,
  They are all to blame, they are all to blame.

'God help me! save I take my part
  Of danger on the roaring sea,
A devil rises in my heart,
  Far worse than any death to me.'

Alfred, Lord Tennyson

When I Set Out for Lyonnesse

When I set out for Lyonnesse,
    A hundred miles away,
    The rime was on the spray,
And starlight lit my lonesomeness
When I set out for Lyonnesse
    A hundred miles away.

What should bechance at Lyonnesse
    While I should sojourn there
    No prophet durst declare,
Nor did the wisest wizard guess
What would bechance at Lyonnesse
    While I should sojourn there.

When I came back from Lyonnesse
    With magic in my eyes,
    All marked with mute surmise
My radiance rare and fathomless,
When I came back from Lyonnesse
    With magic in my eyes!

Thomas Hardy

Babylon

'How many miles to Babylon?'
'Three-score and ten.'
'Can I get there by candle-light?'
'Yes, and back again.'

If your heels are nimble and light,
You may get there by candle-light.

Unknown

Highways and Byways

The Legs

There was this road,
And it led up-hill,
And it led down-hill,
And round and in and out.

And the traffic was legs,
Legs from the knees down,
Coming and going,
Never pausing.

And the gutters gurgled
With the rain's overflow,
And the sticks on the pavement
Blindly tapped and tapped.

What drew the legs along
Was the never-stopping,
And the senseless, frightening
Fate of being legs.

Legs for the road,
The road for legs,
Resolutely nowhere
In both directions.

My legs at least
Were not in that rout:
On grass by the roadside
Entire I stood,

Watching the unstoppable
Legs go by
With never a stumble
Between step and step.

Though my smile was broad
The legs could not see,
Though my laugh was loud
The legs could not hear.

My head dizzicd, then:
I wondered suddenly,
Might I too be a walker
From the knees down?

Gently I touched my shins.
The doubt unchained them:
They had run in twenty puddles
Before I regained them.

Robert Graves

The Footpath Way
from *The Winter's Tale*

Jog on, jog on, the footpath way,
   And merrily hent the stile-a:
A merry heart goes all the day,
   Your sad tires in a mile-a.

William Shakespeare

Tewkesbury Road

It is good to be out on the road, and going one knows
    not where,
    Going through meadow and village, one knows not
    whither nor why;
Through the grey light drift of the dust, in the keen cool
    rush of the air,
    Under the flying white clouds, and the broad blue lift
    of the sky.

And to halt at the chattering brook, in the tall green fern
    at the brink
    Where the harebell grows, and the gorse, and the fox-
    gloves purple and white;
Where the shy-eyed delicate deer come down in a troop to
    drink
    When the stars are mellow and large at the coming on
    of the night.

O, to feel the beat of the rain, and the homely smell of
    the earth,
    Is a tune for the blood to jig to, a joy past power of
    words;
And the blessed green comely meadows are all a-ripple
    with mirth
    At the noise of the lambs at play and the wild cry of
    the birds.

John Masefield

The Little Waves of Breffney

The grand road from the mountain goes shining to the
    sea,
  And there is traffic in it and many a horse and cart,
But the little roads of Cloonagh are dearer far to me,
  And the little roads of Cloonagh go rambling through
    my heart.

A great storm from the ocean goes shouting o'er the hill,
  And there is glory in it and terror on the wind,
But the haunted air of twilight is very strange and still,
  And the little winds of twilight are dearer to my mind.

The great waves of the Atlantic sweep storming on their
    way,
  Shining green and silver with the hidden herring shoal,
But the Little Waves of Breffney have drenched my heart
    in spray.
  And the Little Waves of Breffney go stumbling through
    my soul.

Eva Gore-Booth

Roadways

One road leads to London,
One road runs to Wales,
My road leads me seawards
To the white dipping sails.

    One road leads to the river
    As it goes singing slow;
    My road leads to shipping,
    Where the bronzed sailors go.

Leads me, lures me, calls me
To salt green tossing sea;
A road without earth's road-dust
Is the right road for me.

    A wet road, heaving, shining,
    And wild with seagulls' cries,
    A mad salt sea-wind blowing
    The salt spray in my eyes.

My road calls me, lures me
West, East, South and North;
Most roads lead men homewards,
My road leads me forth –

    To add more miles to the tally
    Of grey miles left behind,
    In quest of that one beauty
    God put me here to find.

John Masefield

Song of the Open Road

I wish to sing the joys of hiking;
It is superior to biking.
I know it is not quite so fast –
That only makes the pleasure last.
Heigh-ho! when springtime is in bud
How jolly then to plough through mud,
To clump along like happy vagrants
And sniff the petrol fumes' sweet fragrance,
As motor cars go flashing past
With honk of horn and klaxon blast.
In winter-time there's nothing like
A good old-fashioned ten-mile hike;
We love to march through rain and sleet
With leaky boots upon our feet,
Our clothes each moment growing wetter,
And if there's hail, that's even better.
And then when summer comes, how gay
Our trek along the broad highway,
With songs upon our dusty lips
And cheery words and merry quips.
When gazing down sweet pastoral vistas
We cannot even think of blisters.
In any weather dry or damp,
There's nothing like a day-long tramp
To make us feel that life is sweet
In spite of corns and aching . . .
Hey, mister, give us a lift!

A. R. D. Fairburn

Changing the Wheel

I sit on the roadside bank.
The driver changes a wheel.
I do not like the place I have come from.
I do not like the place I am going to.
Why do I watch him changing the wheel
With impatience?

Bertolt Brecht
translated from the German by
Michael Hamburger

A Chinese Poem written 1121 BC

White clouds are in the sky.
   Great shoulders of the hills
Between us two must lie.
   The road is rough and far.
   Deep fords between us are.
I pray you not to die.

Translated from the Chinese

The Road Not Taken

Two roads diverged in a yellow wood,
And sorry I could not travel both
And be one traveller, long I stood
And looked down one as far as I could
To where it bent in the undergrowth;

Then took the other, as just as fair,
And having perhaps the better claim,
Because it was grassy and wanted wear;
Though as for that the passing there
Had worn them really about the same,

And both that morning equally lay
In leaves no step had trodden black.
Oh, I kept the first for another day!
Yet knowing how way leads on to way,
I doubted if I should ever come back.

I shall be telling this with a sigh
Somewhere ages and ages hence:
Two roads diverged in a wood, and I –
I took the one less travelled by,
And that has made all the difference.

Robert Frost

Into My Heart an Air that Kills

Into my heart an air that kills
   From yon far country blows:
What are those blue remembered hills,
   What spires, what farms are those?

That is the land of lost content,
   I see it shining plain,
The happy highways where I went
   And cannot come again.

A. E. Housman

A Lonesome Road
from *The Ancient Mariner*

Like one, that on a lonesome road
Doth walk in fear and dread,
And having once turned round walks on,
And turns no more his head;
Because he knows, a frightful fiend
Doth close behind him tread . . .

Samuel Taylor Coleridge

from The End of the Road

In these boots and with this staff
Two hundred leaguers and a half
Walked I, went I, paced I, tripped I,
Marched I, held I, skelped I, slipped I,
Pushed I, panted I, swung and dashed I;
Picked I, forded, swam and splashed I,
Strolled I, climbed I, crawled and scrambled,
Dropped and dipped I, ranged and rambled;
Plodded I, hobbled I, trudged and tramped I,
And in lonely spinnies camped I,
Lingered, loitered, limped and crept I,
Clambered, halted, stepped and leapt I,
Slowly sauntered, roundly strode I,
    And . . .
    Let me not conceal it . . . rode I.

Hilaire Belloc

Fairs, Sports and Games

The Gipsy Girl

'Come, try your skill, kind gentlemen,
    A penny for three tries!'
Some threw and lost, some threw and won
    A ten-a-penny prize.

She was a tawny gipsy girl,
    A girl of twenty years,
I liked her for the lumps of gold
    That jingled from her ears;

I liked the flaring yellow scarf
    Bound loose about her throat,
I liked her showy purple gown
    And flashy velvet coat.

A man came up, too loose of tongue,
    And said no good to her;
She did not blush as Saxons do,
    Or turn upon the cur;

She fawned and whined 'Sweet gentleman,
    A penny for three tries!'
– But oh, the den of wild things in
    The darkness of her eyes!

Ralph Hodgson

A Sheep Fair

The day arrives of the autumn fair,
　　And torrents fall,
Though sheep in throngs are gathered there,
　　Ten thousand all,
Sodden, with hurdles round them reared:
And, lot by lot, the pens are cleared
And the auctioneer wrings out his beard,
And wipes his book, bedrenched and smeared,
And rakes the rain from his face with the edge of his
　　hand,
　　As torrents fall.

Thomas Hardy

The Fair

The Fair is a fight: some are fighting for gain;
Some only for pleasure and some to cheat pain;
But that squinting old hag, with a voice like a knife
And tray of wire monkeys – she's fighting for life.

Eden Phillpots

The Fun Fair

Round about
And round about
And round about we go.
Around the merry roundabout
We're riding high and low.
Our prancing horses leap and bound
And gallop high above the ground
As round about
And round about
And round about we go.

Swinging in the swingboat,
Singing as we go;
Swinging, swinging, swinging,
High and then low.
Swinging to the cloudy sky,
High, low, high.
Swinging to the ground below,
Low, high, low.

The gleaming world begins to reel
As upwards steals the great Big Wheel.
We're slowly lifted through the air,
Until we see the seething Fair,
The stalls, the swings, the streaming people,
Fields and trees, and distant steeple.

Isabel Best

The Fiddler of Dooney

When I play on my fiddle in Dooney
Folk dance like a wave of the sea;
My cousin is priest in Kilvarnet,
My brother in Mocharabuiee.

I passed my brother and cousin:
They read in their books of prayer;
I read in my book of songs
I bought at the Sligo fair.

When we come at the end of time,
To Peter sitting in state,
He will smile on the three old spirits,
But call me first through the gate;

For the good are always the merry,
Save by an evil chance;
And the merry love the fiddle,
And the merry love to dance:

And when the folk there spy me,
They will all come up to me,
With 'Here is the fiddler of Dooney!'
And dance like a wave of the sea.

W. B. Yeats

The Dancing Ploughmen

Rings of stars in sky turns
Above the piper on the hill,
Twelve common clodhopping clowns
About him swing their reel.

One tilts back a foreshortened face
And gazes upwards in a trance
Towards the ring of stars that trace
Upon his eye their ritual dance.

The circling clowns upon the hill
Behind the wheeling fires of space
And moving at an equal pace
See them stand still.

And yet more giddy grows the dance,
The dancers separate and sprawl
And lying prostrate on the grass
Stare upwards at the starry wheel.

M. K. Joseph

A Clownish Song

Trip and go, heave and ho!
Up and down, to and fro,
From the town to the grove,
Two and two let us rove,
A-maying, a-playing;
Love hath no gainsaying.
So merrily trip and go.

Thomas Nashe

The Hunt is Up

The hunt is up! The hunt is up!
   And it is wellnigh day;
And Harry our king is gone hunting,
   To bring the deer to bay.

The east is bright with morning light,
   The darkness it is fled;
The merry horn wakes up the morn
   To leave his idle bed.

Behold the skies with golden dyes
    Are glowing all around;
The grass is green, and so are the treen,
    All laughing at the sound.

The horses snort to hear the sport,
    The dogs are running free,
The woods rejoice at the merry noise
    Of hey tantara tee ree.

The sun is glad to see us clad
    All in our lusty green,
And smiles in the sky as he riseth high
    To see and to be seen.

Awake, all men, I say again,
    Be merry as you may;
For Harry our king is gone hunting
    To bring his deer to bay.

                    Unknown

A Single Hound

When the opal lights in the West had died
   And night was wrapping the red ferns round,
As I came home by the woodland side
   I heard the cry of a single hound.

The huntsman had gathered his pack and gone;
   The last late hoof had echoed away;
The horn was twanging a long way on
   For the only hound that was still astray.

While, heedless of all but the work in hand,
   Up through the brake where the brambles twine,
Crying his joy to a drowsy land
   Javelin drove on a burning line.

The air was sharp with a touch of frost,
   The moon came up like a wheel of gold;
The wall at the end of the woods he crossed
   And flung away on the open wold.

And long as I listened beside the stile
   The larches echoed that eerie sound:
Steady and tireless, mile on mile,
   The hunting cry of a single hound.

Will H. Ogilvie

Winter Shoot
from Windsor Forest

See! from the brake the whirring pheasant springs,
And mounts exulting on triumphant wings;
Short in his joy, he feels the fiery wound,
Flutters in blood, and panting beats the ground.
Ah! what avail his glossy, varying dyes,
His purple crest, and scarlet-circled eyes,
The vivid green his shining plumes unfold,
His painted wings, and breast that flames with gold?

With slaughtering guns the unwearied fowler roves,
When frosts have whitened all the naked groves;
Where doves in flocks the leafless trees o'ershade,
And lonely woodcocks haunt the watery glade.
He lifts the tube,[1] and levels with his eye:
Straight a short thunder breaks the frozen sky.
Oft, as in airy rings they skim the heath,
The clamorous lapwings feel the leaden death:
Oft, as the mounting larks their notes prepare,
They fall, and leave their little lives in air.

Alexander Pope

1. barrel

The Rooks

The bald-faced rooks,
Blown ragged,
Their fingered wings awry,
Harsh-voiced and vengeful
Claw the edge of the gale
And land in a jagged line.

Imperiously
They advance
Over the greening ground,
Dagger heads stabbing
The fragile shoots of wheat
Crouched to earth in the wind.

A shot vibrates.
Abruptly
Their wings blacken the air.
One lifeless comrade
Is left as they cluster
Funereal in the far-off trees.

Albert Rowe

The Boy Fishing

I am cold and alone,
On my tree-root sitting as still as a stone.
The fish come to my net. I scorned the sun,
The voices on the road, and they have gone.
My eyes are buried in the cold pond, under
The cold, spread leaves; my thoughts are silver-wet.
I have ten stickleback, a half-day's plunder,
Safe in my jar. I shall have ten more yet.

E. J. Scovell

Fishing Song

Ragworm, lugworm, mackerel, maggot,
Grey pike lurking, still as steel.
Cast my rod in the deep dark stream
With a nugget of bread for a silver bream.
                            Caught an eel.

Ragworm, lugworm, mackerel, maggot,
Number Ten hook and I'm waiting still.
A carp would be good or a spiny perch,
A golden rudd or a red-finned roach?
                            It's an eel.

Ragworm, lugworm, mackerel, maggot,
Something's biting, wind up the reel!
Is it a pike or a roach or a rudd?
A hunting gudgeon from the river bed?
                            Just – an eel.

Judith Nicholls

Floating on the Jo Yeh Stream in Spring

Here is seclusion and stillness with nothing to break the
     spell;
We follow wherever the boat chooses to drift;
The evening wind wafts it on its way
Entering the mouth of the gorge between flowery paths,
As dusk falls we wind among the western ravines.
Through a break in the hills one can see the Southern
     Dipper.
The air is heavy with floating mist
The moon among the trees sinks at my back.
The life of the world of men is a boundless waste;
My wish is to spend my days here as a fisherman in wild
     places.

Chi Wu-Ch'ien
8th century, translated
from the Chinese by
Soames Jenyns

Starfish

Went star-fishing last night.
Dipped my net in the inky lake
to catch a star for my collection.
All I did was splintered the moon.

Judith Nicholls

To a Squirrel at Kyle-na-no

Come play with me;
Why should you run
Through the shaking tree
As though I'd a gun
To strike you dead?
When all I would do
Is to scratch your head
And let you go.

W. B. Yeats

Day by Day I Float My Paper Boats

Day by day I float my paper boats one by one down the
running stream.
In big black letters I write my name on them and the
name of the village where I live.
I hope that someone in some strange land will find them
and know who I am.
I load my little boats with shiuli flowers from our
garden, and hope that these blooms of the dawn will
be carried safely to land in the night . . .

Rabindranath Tagore

Boy With Kite

I am master of my kite, and
the wind tugs against me
on blue ropes of air.
Above tasselled trees
my kite glides and swoops,
pink-and-yellow falcon surging loose
from my tight fist.
White string bites
into flesh; my wrist
flexes like a falconer's.

I am dancing with my kite
heel-and-toe to earth,
body braced
against the fleet north-easter, laced
with fraying clouds.

Looking up,
lifted steeple-clear
of church and school and hill,
I am master of my world.

Phoebe Hesketh

The Midnight Skaters

The hop-poles stand in cones,
　　The icy pond lurks under,
The pole-tops steeple to the thrones
　　Of stars, sound gulfs of wonder;
But not the tallest there, 'tis said,
Could fathom to this pond's black bed.

Then is not death at watch
　　Within those secret waters?
What wants he but to catch
　　Earth's heedless sons and daughters?
With but a crystal parapet
Between, he has his engines set.

Then on, blood shouts, on, on,
　　Twirl, wheel and whip above him,
Dance on this ball-floor thin and wan,
　　Use him as though you love him;
Court him, elude him, reel and pass,
And let him hate you through the glass.

Edmund Blunden

Skating
from *The Prelude*

And in the frosty season, when the sun
Was set, and visible for many a mile
The cottage windows blazed through twilight gloom,
I heeded not their summons: happy time
It was indeed for all of us – for me
It was a time of rapture! Clear and loud
The village clock tolled six, – I wheeled about,
Proud and exulting like an untired horse
That cares not for his home. All shod with steel,
We hissed along the polished ice in games
Confederate, imitative of the chase
And woodland pleasures, – the resounding horn,
The pack loud chiming, and the hunted hare.
So through the darkness and the cold we flew,
And not a voice was idle; with the din
Smitten, the precipices rang aloud;
The leafless trees and every icy crag
Tinkled like iron; while far distant hills
Into the tumult sent an alien sound
Of melancholy not unnoticed, while the stars
Eastward were sparkling clear, and in the west
The orange sky of evening died away.
Not seldom from the uproar I retired
Into a silent bay, or sportively
Glanced sideway, leaving the tumultuous throng,
To cut across the reflex of a star
That fled, and, flying still before me, gleamed
Upon the glassy plain; and oftentimes,
When we had given our bodies to the wind,
And all the shadowy banks on either side

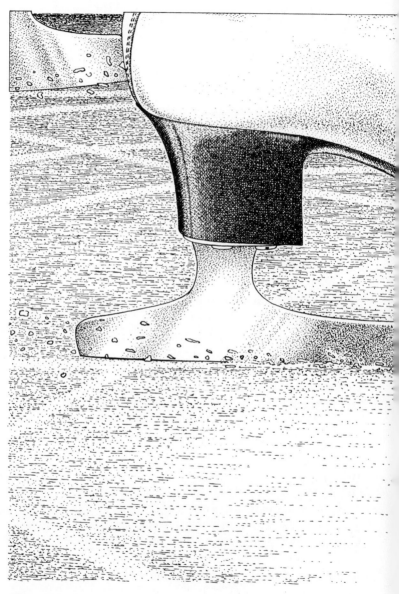

Came sweeping through the darkness, spinning still
The rapid line of motion, then at once
Have I, reclining back upon my heels,
Stopped short; yet still the solitary cliffs
Wheeled by me – even as if the earth had rolled
With visible motion her diurnal round!
Behind me did they stretch in solemn train,
Feebler and feebler, and I stood and watched
Till all was tranquil as a dreamless sleep.

William Wordsworth

from The Bells

Hear the sledges with the bells –
   Silver bells!
What a world of merriment their melody foretells!
   How they tinkle, tinkle, tinkle,
      In the icy air of night!
   While the stars, that oversprinkle
   All the heavens, seem to twinkle
      With a crystalline delight;
   Keeping time, time, time,
   In a sort of Runic rhyme,
To the tintinnabulation that so musically wells
   From the bells, bells, bells, bells,
         Bells, bells, bells –
From the jingling and the tinkling of the bells.

Edgar Allan Poe

The Game . . . at the Hallowe'en Party in Hangman's Wood

Around the trees ran witches
   Their nails as long as knives.
Behind a bush hid demons
   In fear for their lives.

       Murder, murder in the dark!
       The screams ring in your ears.
       It's just a game, a silly lark,
       No need for floods of tears.

Tall ghosts and other nasties
   Jumped out and wailed like trains.
A skeleton in irons
   Kept rattling his chains.

       Murder, murder in the dark!
       The screams ring in your ears.
       It's just a game, a silly lark,
       So wipe away those tears.

A werewolf howled his heart out;
   The Horrid Dwarf crept by.
There was blood upon his boots
   And murder in his eye.

       Murder, murder in the dark!
       The screams ring in your ears.
       It's just a game, a silly lark,
       Oh, come now, no more tears.

Owls were hooting, 'Is it you?'
    Until a wizard grim
Pointed to the Dwarf and said,
    'The murderer . . . it's him!'

            Murder, murder in the dark!
            The screams ring in your ears.
            It's just a game, a silly lark,
            There's no time left for tears.

Murder, murder in the dark!
The screams fade in the night.
Listen, there's a farm dog's bark!
And look, the dawn's first light!

                    Wes Magee

Nurse's Song

When the voices of the children are heard on the
      green,
    And laughing is heard on the hill,
My heart is at rest within my breast,
    And everything else is still.

'Then come home, my children, the sun is gone
           down,
     And the dews of night arise;
Come, come, leave off play, and let us away,
     Till the morning appears in the skies.'

'No, no, let us play, for it is yet day,
     And we cannot go to sleep;
Besides, in the sky the little birds fly,
     And the hills are all covered with sheep.'

'Well, well, go and play till the light fades away,
     And then go home to bed.'
The little ones leaped, and shouted, and laughed,
     And all the hills echoèd.

William Blake

The Country Life

Clearing at Dawn

The fields are chill, the sparse rain has stopped;
The colours of Spring teem on every side.
With leaping fish the blue pond is full;
With singing thrushes the green boughs droop.
The flowers of the field have dabbled their powdered
    cheeks;
The mountain grasses are bent level at the waist.
By the bamboo stream the last fragment of cloud
Blown by the wind slowly scatters away.

Li Po
translated from the Chinese by
Arthur Waley

The Lark in the Morning

As I was a-walking
One morning in spring,
I heard a pretty ploughboy,
So sweetly he did sing;
And as he was a-singing
These words I heard him say:
'Oh, there's no life like the ploughboy
All in the month of May.'

There's the lark in the morning
She will rise up from her nest,
She'll mount the white air
With the dew on her breast,
And with the pretty ploughboy O,
She'll whistle and she'll sing,
And at night she'll return
To her nest back again.

Unknown

The Country Lad

Who can live in heart so glad
As the merry country lad?
Who upon a fair green balk[1]
May at pleasure sit and walk,
And amid the azure skies
See the morning sun arise,
While he hears in every spring
How the birds do chirp and sing:

Or before the hounds in cry
See the hare go stealing by:
Or along the shallow brook,
Angling with a baited hook,
See the fishes leap and play
In a blessed sunny day:
Or to hear the partridge call
Till she have her covey[2] all:
Or to see the subtle fox,
How the villain plies the box;[3]
After feeding on his prey,
How he closely sneaks away,
Through the hedge and down the furrow
Till he gets into his burrow:
Then the bee to gather honey;
And the little black-haired coney,[4]
On a bank for sunny place,
With her forefeet wash her face, –
Are not these, with thousands moe
Than the courts of kings do know,
The true pleasing spirit's sights
That may breed true love's delights?

Nicholas Breton

1. bank 2. brood 3. raids the chicken run 4. rabbit

The Cock is Crowing

The Cock is crowing,
The stream is flowing,
The small birds twitter,
The lake doth glitter,
The green field sleeps in the sun:
The oldest and youngest
Are at work with the strongest;
The cattle are grazing,
Their heads never raising;
There are forty feeding like one!

Like an army defeated
The snow hath retreated,
And now doth fare ill
On the top of the bare hill;
The Ploughboy is whooping – anon – anon:
There's joy in the mountains;
There's life in the fountains;
Small clouds are sailing,
Blue sky prevailing;
The rain is over and gone!

William Wordsworth

Farm Scene

They come each morning to the gate,
Are milked, and wander off to feed;
Six cows, a calf, and in the lead
A brindled bull, old, fat, sedate.

And every evening they are back,
Loafing along the quarter-mile
Of dusty lane in single file,
The old bull trailing up the track.

I would not load with thought that brings
Meanings deep-conjured in the mind
This quiet scene – but here I find
The rhythm of eternal things,

And envy him who takes his pail
Jingling to meet them at the gate;
Sun-up, sun-down, that constant date
Which neither he nor they will fail.

I envy him whose life allows
Him this cool blessedness: to stand
And simply watch the coming and
Later the going of the cows.

Ernest G. Moll

Happiness

When I, but hedge-high
And meadow-sweet tall
Rambled the countryside,
My nose,
Gay with the sweet smell
Of bramble and briar,
The rose of the hedgerows
        all mine,
And the powder of moth-wing and butterfly,
Motes in the lanes of the sun –
        All was well.
The fire of distant stars in the night
Was also my height,
And the rocket of rooks shot into the sky
Fell back on to earth, my playthings . . . I feel
O then there were skies to swim
And great seas to fly, and heaven was on the ground,
My paradise all found . . . .
And I did not need to kneel.

                    Erica Marx

Around Sheepwash

Walking along these lanes again,
counting the trees in the hedgerows – hazel,
willow, bramble, honeysuckle, oak
(still leafless this, but the cork marbles
betrayed it), blackthorn in smudgy flower,
and the holly and the ivy – the carol came
irresistibly – I passed these things:
a black and white goose, cosy-catlike
on a cottage doorstep (I stared and smiled);
a half-grown puppy (I played solemn,
sent it sternly home); two lambs
loose outside a gate with a gap
(I tiptoed past, not to frighten them,
leaving their mothers to baa them back);
a thatched barn deep in a hollow
at a curve in the lane, its door furry
with the dangling tails of slaughtered vermin
(I puzzled over them, teasing after
the shapes of the bodies that had borne them);
then slow solitudes of hawk and cloud,
wind in thickets, the sun westering;
and half a mile before the village,
near the river, on the roadside verge,
a girl's coat, well-made, slim-waisted,
spread on its back, sleeves tidy,
primroses tucked into one pocket;
stark empty. And I hastened my steps.

Fleur Adcock

The Greenwood Tree
from *As You Like It*

Under the greenwood tree,
Who loves to lie with me,
And turn his merry note
Unto the sweet bird's throat,
Come hither, come hither, come hither;
     Here shall he see
     No enemy,
But winter and rough weather.

Who doth ambition shun
And loves to lie in the sun,
Seeking the food he eats,
And pleased with what he gets,
Come hither, come hither, come hither;
     Here shall he see
     No enemy,
But winter and rough weather.

           William Shakespeare

The Cloud – Mobile

Above my face is a map,
Continents form and fade.
Blue countries, made
on a white sea, are erased,
and white countries traced
on a blue sea.

It is a map that moves,
faster than real,
but so slow.
Only my watching proves
that island has being,
or that bay.

It is a model of time.
Mountains are wearing away,
coasts cracking,
the ocean spills over,
then new hills
heap into view
with river-cuts of blue
between them.

It is a map of change.
This is the way things are
with a stone or a star.
This is the way things go,
hard or soft,
swift or slow.

                    May Swenson

Joys

We may shut our eyes,
But we cannot help knowing
That skies are clear
And grass is growing;
The breeze comes whispering in our ear,
That dandelions are blossoming near,
That corn has sprouted,
That streams are flowing,
That the river is bluer than the sky,
That the robin is plastering his home hard by.

James Russell Lowell

from I am the One

I am the one whom ringdoves see
      Through chinks in boughs
      When they do not rouse
      In sudden dread,
But stay on cooing, as if they said:
      'Oh; it's only he.'

I am the passer when up-eared hares,
      Stirred as they eat
      The new-sprung wheat,
      Their munch resume
As if they thought: 'He is one for whom
      Nobody cares.'

Thomas Hardy

Wiltshire Downs

The cuckoo's double note
Loosened like bubbles from a drowning throat
Floats through the air
In a mockery of pipit, lark and stare.

The stable-boys thud by
Their horses slinging divots at the sky
And with bright hooves
Printing the sodden turf with lucky grooves.

As still as a windhover
A shepherd in his flapping coat leans over
His tall sheep-crook
And shearlings, tegs and yoes[1] cons like a book.

And one tree-crowned long barrow
Stretched like a sow that has brought forth her farrow
Hides a king's bones
Lying like broken sticks among the stones.

Andrew Young

1. different kinds of sheep

The Thresher
from *The Task*

Between the upright shafts of those tall elms
We may discern the thresher at his task.
Thump after thump, resounds the constant flail,
That seems to swing uncertain, and yet falls
Full on the destined ear. Wide flies the chaff;
The rustling straw sends up a frequent mist
Of atoms, sparkling in the noon-day beam.

William Cowper

In a Cornfield

A silence of full noontide heat
Grew on them at their toil:
The farmer's dog woke up from sleep,
The green snake hid her coil
Where grass grew thickest; bird and beast
Sought shadows as they could,
The reaping men and women paused
And sat down where they stood;
They ate and drank and were refreshed,
For rest from toil is good.

Christina Rossetti

High on the Hill

High on the hill I can see it all,
the anthill men and the doll's house town,
the bowl of sea and the trim toy ships.
Here only the trees at hand are tall.

High on the hill I can touch a cloud
or measure miles with my fingertips,
can hide the town with a palm turned down
and drown its noise when I speak aloud.

High on the hill it's all a joke
and I wonder why I bothered at all
with the clockwork cars and the anthill folk
that height and distance make so small.

Tom Wright

From a Valley

High overhead the marksman hawk,
Sharpshooting in the pass,
Sees plover, snipe and pipit burst
Like buckshot from the grass.

The catapulted curlews dive,
Lamenting as they go,
Down the great quadrant of the wind
To a world's end below.

But quiet men of middle-earth
Moon homeward, unaware
Of how the black formations mass
In windy middle-air.

Across this tapestry of trees
The fading sunlight steals,
And wagtails glide about the lawn
As though on little wheels.

Paul Dehn

Windy Gap

As I was going through Windy Gap
A hawk and a cloud hung over the map.

The land lay bare and the wind blew loud
And the hawk cried out from the heart of the cloud,

'Before I fold my wings in sleep
I'll pick the bones of your travelling sheep,

For the leaves blow black and the wintry sun
Shows the trees' white skeleton.'

A magpie sat in the tree's high top
Singing a song on Windy Gap

That streamed far down to the plain below
Like a shaft of light from a high window.

From the bending tree he sang aloud,
And the sun shone out of the heart of the cloud.

And it seemed to me as we travelled through
That my sheep were the notes that trumpet blew.

And so I sing this song of praise
For travelling sheep and blowing days.

                              David Campbell

Blows the Wind

Blows the wind today, and the sun and the rain are flying,
  Blows the wind on the moors today and now,
Where about the graves of the martyrs the whaups are
      crying,   *curlews*
  My heart remembers how!

Grey recumbent tombs of the dead in desert places,
　　Standing stones on the vacant wine-red moor,
Hills of sheep, and the howes of the silent vanished races,
　　And winds, austere and pure.

Be it granted me to behold you again in dying,
　　Hills of home! and to hear again the call;
Hear about the graves of the martyrs the peewees crying,
　　And hear no more at all.

Robert Louis Stevenson

Landscape as Werewolf

Near here, the last grey wolf
In England was clubbed down. Still,
After two hundred years, the same pinched wind
Rakes through his cairn of bones

As he squats quiet, watching daylight seep
Away from the scarred granite, and its going drain
The hills' bare faces. Far below,
A tiny bus twists on its stringy path
And scuttles home around a darkening bend.

The fells contract, regroup in starker forms;
Dusk tightens on them, as the wind gets up
And stretches hungrily: tensed at the nape,
The coarse heath bristles like a living pelt.

The sheep are all penned in. Down at the pub
They sing, and shuttle darts: the hostellers
Dubbin their heavy boots. Above the crags
The first stars prick their eyes and bide their time.

William Dunlop

Plucking the Rushes

Green rushes with red shoots,
Long leaves bending to the wind –
You and I in the same boat
Plucking rushes at the Five Lakes.
We started at dawn from the orchid-island:
We rested under the elms till noon.
You and I plucking rushes
Had not plucked a handful when night came!

Unknown
4th century translated
from the Chinese by
Arthur Waley

Dreamer's Autumn

The croaking crows fly home at eventide;
My heart to them I've long thrown open wide.

Autumn its sadness to the wanderer brings
– Fields without flowers and woods where no bird sings –

But in the village all is gay; the men
Have gathered in their crops and sown again.

Alone, around the neighbours' farms I steal;
Silent, I watch the joys that others feel,

And to the croaking crows at eventide
My heart, as always, is thrown open wide.

V. Dyk
translated from the Czech by
E. Osers and J. K. Montgomery

There was a Boy
from *The Prelude*

There was a boy; ye knew him well, ye cliffs
And islands of Winander! – many a time,
At evening, when the earliest stars began
To move along the edges of the hills,
Rising or setting, would he stand alone,
Beneath the trees, or by the glimmering lake;
And there, with fingers interwoven, both hands
Pressed closely palm to palm and to his mouth
Uplifted, he, as through an instrument,
Blew mimic hootings to the silent owls,
That they might answer him. – And they would
   shout
Across the watery vale, and shout again,
Responsive to his call, – with quivering peals,
And long halloos, and screams, and echoes loud
Redoubled and redoubled; concourse wild
Of jocund din! And, when there came a pause
Of silence such as baffled his best skill:
Then, sometimes, in that silence, while he hung
Listening, a gentle shock of mild surprise
Has carried far into his heart the voice
Of mountain-torrents; or the visible scene
Would enter unawares into his mind
With all its solemn imagery, its rocks,
Its woods, and that uncertain heaven received
Into the bosom of the steady lake.

William Wordsworth

The Harvest Moon

The flame-red moon, the harvest moon,
Rolls along the hills, gently bouncing,
A vast balloon,
Till it takes off, and sinks upward
To lie in the bottom of the sky, like a gold doubloon.

The harvest moon has come,
Booming softly through heaven, like a bassoon.
And earth replies all night, like a deep drum.

So people can't sleep,
So they go out where elms and oak trees keep
A kneeling vigil, in a religious hush.
The harvest moon has come!

And all the moonlit cows and all the sheep
Stare up at her petrified, while she swells
Filling heaven, as if red hot, and sailing
Closer and closer like the end of the world

Till the gold fields of stiff wheat
Cry 'We are ripe, reap us!' and the rivers
Sweat from the melting hills.

Ted Hughes

The Farmer

Star-mist was on the hills; the cows had been fed.
It was twilight, soft and windless,
and the trees in the west tipped with red.
I walked with the farmer through the fallows,
while the dogs drove the sheep ahead.
We had to shout in that babble of lambs bleating
in long bursts of hunger that fell into hushes,
while the ewes ran from lamb to lamb frenziedly
      sniffing,
searching with strange little rushes,
and the rams turned to stamp at the dogs.
And though I had lived with the man in his home,
seen him a thousand times with his children and wife,
I had not known before such tenderness to come
into his face as he raised a sick lamb from its rest
and, folding its forelegs gently, carried it close to his
      breast.

Flexmore Hudson

A Child's Voice

On winter nights shepherd and I
   Down to the lambing shed would go;
Rain round our swinging lamp did fly
   Like shining flakes of snow.

There on a nail our lamp we hung,
   And O it was beyond belief
To see those ewes lick with hot tongues
   The limp wet lambs to life.

A week gone and sun shining warm
   It was as good as gold to hear
Those new-born voices round the farm
   Cry shivering and clear.

Where was a prouder man than I
   Who knew the night those lambs were born
Watching them leap two feet on high
   And stamp the ground in scorn?

Gone sheep and shed and lighted rain
   And blue March morning; yet today
A small voice crying brings again
   Those lambs leaping at play.

Andrew Young

Dusk

The dark night falling silent   mist
     Obscuring Snowdon,
The sun in its bed of sea water
And the moon silvering the waves.

Walter Davies
(Gwallter Mechain)
translated from the Welsh by
Aran John

Summer Night

As we walk, the moon ahead of us
Appears to be falling through
Each tree we pass, and sieves
Star after star through screens
Of thickening leaves.

The green hedge is wider now
With white may, hanging grass. The chestnut
Trims itself with pink and snowy cones;
The moon as we walk drops through each tree
And scatters silvery grit among the country stones.

James Kirkup

Vagabonds
and Wanderers

The Vagabond

Give to me the life I love,
   Let the lave [1] go by me,
Give the jolly heaven above
   And the byway nigh me.
Bed in the bush with stars to see,
   Bread I dip in the river –
There's the life for a man like me,
   There's the life for ever.

Let the blow fall soon or late,
   Let what will be o'er me;
Give the face of earth around
   And the road before me.
Wealth I seek not, hope nor love,
   Nor a friend to know me;
All I seek, the heaven above
   And the road below me.

Or let autumn fall on me
    Where afield I linger,
Silencing the bird on tree,
    Biting the blue finger.
White as meal the frosty field –
    Warm the fireside haven –
Not to autumn will I yield,
    Not to winter even!

Let the blow fall soon or late,
    Let what will be o'er me;
Give the face of earth around
    And the road before me.
Wealth I ask not, hope nor love,
    Nor a friend to know me;
All I ask, the heaven above
    And the road below me.

Robert Louis Stevenson

1. rest, remainder

A Vagabond Song

There is something in the autumn that is native to my
  blood –
Touch of manner, hint of mood;
And my heart is like a rhyme,
With the yellow and the purple and the crimson keeping
  time.

The scarlet of the maples can shake me like a cry
Of bugles going by.
And my lonely spirit thrills
To see the frosty asters like a smoke upon the hills.

There is something in October sets the gypsy blood astir;
We must rise and follow her,
When from every hill of flame
She calls and calls each vagabond by name.

Bliss Carman

Gipsies

The gipsies seek wide sheltering woods again,
With droves of horses flock to mark their lane,
And trample on dead leaves, and hear the sound,
And look and see the black clouds gather round,
And set their camps, and free from muck and mire,
And gather stolen sticks to make the fire.
The roasted hedgehog, bitter though as gall,
Is eaten up and relished by them all.
They know the woods and every fox's den
And get their living far away from men;
The shooters ask them where to find the game,
The rabbits know them and are almost tame.
The aged women, tawny with the smoke,
Go with the winds and crack the rotted oak.

John Clare

Gypsy Dance

I saw the gypsy queen
Dancing the flamenco,
Her flowing skirts changing, luminous in the light of the
    fire,
That rough black flowing mane twisting.
She jumped,
Oh how she jumped over that bitter roaring fire.
All the gypsy folk,
Their faces black in the shadows,
Waited.
Then, she fell on her knees
As though she were praying to God in the highest.
Oh how the gypsy folk clapped.
They clapped as hard as the moon shone.

Linda Davies
aged eleven

Meg Merrilies

Old Meg she was a Gipsy,
    And lived upon the Moors:
Her bed it was the brown heath turf,
    And her house was out of doors.

Her apples were swart blackberries,
    Her currants pods o' broom;
Her wine was dew of the wild white rose,
    Her book a churchyard tomb.

Her Brothers were the craggy hills,
    Her Sisters larchen trees;
Alone with her great family
    She lived as she did please.

No breakfast had she many a morn,
    No dinner many a noon,
And 'stead of supper she would stare
    Full hard against the Moon.

But every morn of woodbine fresh
    She made her garlanding,
And every night the dark glen Yew
    She wove, and she would sing.

And with her fingers old and brown,
    She plaited Mats o' Rushes,
And gave them to the Cottagers
    She met among the Bushes.

Old Meg was brave as Margaret Queen,
    And tall as Amazon;
An old red blanket cloak she wore,
    A chip hat had she on:
God rest her agèd bones somewhere –
    She died full long agone!

John Keats

An Old Woman of the Road

O, to have a little house!
To own the hearth and stool and all!
The heaped-up sods upon the fire,
The pile of turf against the wall!

To have a clock with weights and chains
And pendulum swinging up and down!
A dresser filled with shining delph,
Speckled and white and blue and brown!

I could be busy all the day
Clearing and sweeping hearth and floor,
And fixing on their shelf again
My white and blue and speckled store!

I could be quiet then at night
Beside the fire and by myself,
Sure of a bed, and loth to leave
The ticking clock and the shining delph!

Och! but I'm weary of mist and dark,
And roads where there's never a house or bush
And tired I am of bog and road
And the crying wind and the lonesome hush.

And I am praying to God on high,
And I am praying Him night and day,
For a little house – a house of my own –
Out of the wind's and the rain's way.

Padraic Colum

Minstrel

The road unravels as I go,
walking into the sun, the anaemic
sun that lights Van Diemen's Land.
This week I have sung for my supper in seven towns.
I sleep in haysheds and corners
out of the wind, wrapped in a Wagga Rug.
In the mornings pools of mist fragment the country,
bits of field are visible higher up on ridges,
treetops appear, the mist hangs about for hours.
A drink at a valley river coming down
out of Mount Ossa; climb back to the road,
start walking, a song to warm these lips
whitebitten with cold.
In the hedges live tiny birds
who sing in bright colours you would not hear
from your fast vehicles. They sing for minstrels
and the sheep. The wires sing, too, with the wind;
also the leaves; it is not lonely.

Michael Dransfield

Madly Singing in the Mountains

There is no one among men that has not a special failing:
And my failing consists of writing verses.
I have broken away from the thousand ties of life:
But this infirmity still remains behind.
Each time that I look at a fine landscape,
Each time that I meet a loved friend,
I raise my voice and recite a stanza of poetry
And I am glad as though a God had crossed my path.
Ever since the day I was banished to Hsün-yang
Half my time I have lived among the hills.
Often, when I have finished a new poem
Alone I climb the road to the Eastern Rock.
I lean my body on the banks of white stone:
I pull down with my hands a green cassia branch.
My mad singing startles the valleys and hills;
The apes and birds all come to peep.
Fearing to become a laughing stock to the world,
I choose a place that is unfrequented by men.

Po Chü-i
translated from the Chinese by
Arthur Waley

Beachcomber

Monday I found a boot –
Rust and salt leather.
I gave it back to the sea, to dance in.

Tuesday a spar of timber worth thirty bob.
Next winter
It will be a chair, a coffin, a bed.

Wednesday a half can of Swedish spirits.
I tilted my head.
The shore was cold with mermaids and angels.

Thursday I got nothing, seaweed,
A whale bone,
Wet feet and a loud cough.

Friday I held a seaman's skull,
Sand spilling from it
The way time is told on kirkyard stones.

Saturday a barrel of sodden oranges.
A Spanish ship
Was wrecked last month at The Kame.

Sunday, for fear of the elders,
I sit on my bum.
What's heaven? A sea chest with a thousand
    gold coins.

George Mackay Brown

Harry Pearce

I sat beside the red stock route
   And chewed a blade of bitter grass
And saw in mirage on the plain
   A bullock wagon pass.
Old Harry Pearce was with his team.
'The flies are bad,' I said to him.

The leaders felt his whip. It did
   Me good to hear old Harry swear
And in the heat of noon it seemed
   His bullocks walked on air.
Suspended in the amber sky
They hauled the wool to Gundagai.

He walked in Time across the plain,
   An old man walking in the air.
For years he wandered in my brain;
   And now he lodges here.
And he may drive his cattle still
When Time with us has had his will.

David Campbell

Tramp

I could see he was a bearded brigand
With a fierce, full spade
Of whiskers,
Bush-ranger hat
And sleeveless, leather jacket.

The dry twigs underneath the hedge
Cracked, writhed and twisted
In the red-hot wigwam of his healing fire.
Underpants and vest
Hung on a thin, stretched line
Over the halberds [1] of the yellow flames,
Trousers softening to dryness on his hairy legs,
Feet simmering in the sweat of steaming socks.

It will rain,
The bundles of the black, low clouds make sure.
But in the spinney is a simple hut,
An oilskin roof,
Some plastic bags,
Dry sacks,
And purring on the fire a pan
For cocoa
And a stone bed-bottle.

But all too soon,
Hours before yellow dawn lights up the fret
Of branches in the hedge,
His knees will lock with cold;
The fire will settle into grey, wet ash.
A spinney is a harsh, bleak place
To lie
All night in rain.

And in the morning
He will stagger through stiffness,
Lean on the handles of the grubby pram
Stuffed with his clothes, his bedding
And his clanking pans.
His medals tinkle on their faded silks,
And sometimes he will talk
Of this campaign or that –
Nothing heroic,
He was there, that's all.
And by his accent and his ready words
There are romantics who would judge him
Class,
College at least perhaps, or university –
A sort of scholar gipsy.

One day,
Savaged by freedom
Turned to a snarling master,
They found him by the tyrant,
Stretched in a ditch –
One afternoon
A farm-hand and a policeman on patrol
Stood by the shrunken foetus,
Waxen, already cold,
Beard still defiant in sleep.

Gregory Harrison

1. Combined spear and battle-axe

The Little Cart

The little cart jolting and banging through the yellow
    haze of dusk;
The man pushing behind, the woman pulling in front.
They have left the city and do not know where to go.
'Green green, those elm-tree leaves; they will cure my
    hunger.
If only we could find some quiet place and sup on them
    together.'

The wind has flattened the yellow mother-wort;
Above it in the distance they see walls of a house.
'There surely must be people living who'll give you
    something to eat.'
They tap at the door, but no one comes; they look in, but
    the kitchen is empty.
They stand hesitating in the lonely road and their tears
    fall like rain.

Ch'ên Tsǔ-Lung
translated from the Chinese by
Arthur Waley

from The Seafarer

Prosperous men,
Living on land, do not begin to understand
How I, careworn and cut off from my kinsmen,
Have as an exile endured the winter
On the icy sea . . .
Icicles hung round me; hail showers flew.
The only sound here, was of the sea booming –
The ice-cold wave – and at times the song of the swan.
The cry of the gannet was all my gladness,
The call of the curlew, not the laughter of men,
The mewing gull, not the sweetness of mead.
There, storms echoed off the rocky cliffs; the icy-feathered
   tern
Answered them; and often the eagle,
Dewy-winged, screeched overhead.

Unknown
translated from the Anglo-Saxon by
Kevin Crossley-Holland

The Dying Hobo

Beside a western tank,
One cold November day;
Sheltered by a box car
The dying hobo lay.

His partner sat beside him
And slowly stroked his head;
As he listened to the last words
The dying hobo said.

'I'm going to a better land,
Where everything is bright;
Where handouts grow on bushes
And you sleep out every night.

'Where a man don't ever have to work,
Or even change his socks;
And little streams of whiskey
Come trickling down the rocks.

'Just tell my girl in Denver,
Her face no more I'll view,
For I'm going to hop a fast freight
And ride her right straight through.'

His eyes grew dim, his head fell back,
He'd sung his last refrain,
His partner hooked his coat and pants,
And caught an eastbound train.

Unknown

The Dead Swagman

His rusted billy left beside the tree;
Under a root, most carefully tucked away,
His steel-rimmed glasses folded in their case
Of mildewed purple velvet; there he lies
In the sunny afternoon and takes his ease,
Curled like a possum within the hollow trunk.

He came one winter evening when the tree
Hunched its broad back against the rain, and made
His camp, and slept, and did not wake again.
Now white ants make a home within his skull:
His old friend Fire has walked across the hill
And blackened the old tree and the old man
And buried him half in ashes, where he lay.

It might be called a lonely death. The tree
Had its own alien life beneath the sun,
Yet both belong to the Bush, and now are one:
The roots and bones lie close among the soil,
And he ascends in leaves towards the sky.

Nancy Cato

Adventure

from The Call of the Wild

They have cradled you in custom, they have primed you
   with their preaching,
  They have soaked you in convention through and
   through;
They have put you in a showcase; you're a credit to their
   teaching –
  But can't you hear the Wild? – it's calling you.
Let us probe the silent places, let us seek what luck betide
   us;
  Let us journey to a lonely land I know.
There's a whisper on the night-wind, there's a star agleam
   to guide us,
  And the Wild is calling, calling . . . let us go.

R. W. Service

The Song of the Ungirt Runners

We swing ungirded hips,
And lightened are our eyes,
The rain is on our lips,
We do not run for prize.
We know not whom we trust
Nor whitherward we fare,
But we run because we must
　　Through the great wide air.

The waters of the seas
Are troubled as by storm.
The tempest strips the trees
And does not leave them warm.
Does the tearing tempest pause?
Do the tree-tops ask it why?
So we run without a cause
　　'Neath the big bare sky.

The rain is on our lips,
We do not run for prize.
But the storm the water whips
And the wave howls to the skies.

The winds arise and strike it
And scatter it like sand,
And we run because we like it
　　Through the broad bright land.

C. H. Sorley

Wanderlust

There are times I have to wander, when the wild breeze
　　fans my hair,
And the veld is calling to me; and the great lion roars in
　　its lair,
Its voice a peal of thunder, and its head raised to the sky;
And the quiet is torn asunder till the throbbing echoes
　　die . . .

And my wanderlust is calling, it is calling me away,
And when wanderlust is calling, then I cannot disobey . . .
And when wanderlust is calling, then my blood is burning
high,
For I love the starry silence and the dark African sky;
And I love the placid river, and the great lion's shaggy
mane,
And my wanderlust is calling: I shall see those things
again.
When my wanderlust is calling, then I see the
mountains blue
And the blesbok[1] and the great-eyed gazelles of
the wild Karoo;
And the deepness and the darkness and the beauty
of the night,
And the freshness and the fairness of the dawn and of the
light.
Then I smell the orange blossoms and I feel the sun's
warm rays,
And a yearning comes within me for those happy
wander days;
And I think of lonely rivers and great mountains capped
with snow,
And I think of my Africa, and I murmur very low:
'I am going, I am going, I am going far away
For my wanderlust is calling and I dare not disobey.'

Elizabeth Du Preez
aged twelve

1. large South African antelope

On the Veld

The red flame-flowers bloom and die,
The embers puff a golden spark,
Now and again a horse's eye
Shines like a topaz in the dark.

A distant jackal jars the hush,
The drowsy oxen champ and sigh,
The ghost moon peers above the bush
And creeps across the starry sky.

Crosbie Garstin

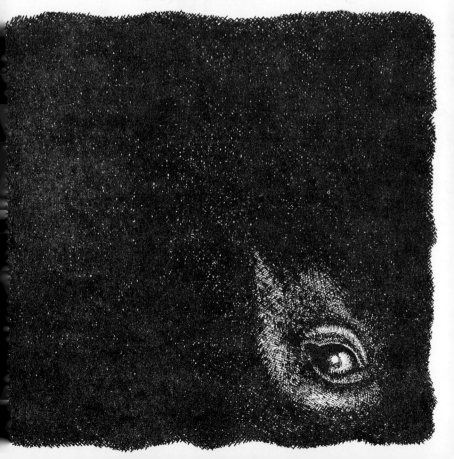

On the Congo

Our ship, the Sea Smithy, swerved out of the tradewinds
and began to creep up the Congo River.
Vines trailed along the deck like ropes.
We met the famous iron barges of the Congo,
whose hot steeldecks swarmed with negroes from the
    tributaries.

They put their hands to their mouths
and shouted, 'Go to hell' in a Bantu language.
We slid marvelling and depressed through the tunnels of
    vegetation
and cook in his galley thought:
'Now I am peeling potatoes in the middle of the Congo.'

At night the Sea Smithy
goggled with its red eyes into the jungle,
an animal roared, a jungle rat plopped into the water,
a millet mortar coughed sharply,
and a drum was beating softly in a village somewhere
    where the rubber negroes were going on with their
    slave lives.

Harry Edmund Martinson
translated from the Swedish by
Robert Bly

135

The Jungle Husband

Dearest Evelyn, I often think of you
Out with the guns in the jungle stew
Yesterday I hittapotamus
I put the measurements down for you but they got lost in
    the fuss
It's not a good thing to drink out here
You know, I've practically given it up dear.
Tomorrow I am going alone a long way
Into the jungle. It is all grey
But green on top
Only sometimes when a tree has fallen
The sun comes down plop, it is quite appalling.
You never want to go in a jungle pool
In the hot sun, it would be the act of a fool
Because it's always full of anacondas, Evelyn, not looking
    ill-fed
I'll say. So no more now, from your loving husband,
    Wilfred.

Stevie Smith

Good Taste

Travelling, a man met a tiger, so . . .
He ran. The tiger ran after him
Thinking: How fast I run . . . But

The road thought: How long I am . . . Then,
They came to a cliff, yes, the man
Grabbed at an ash root and swung down

Over its edge. Above his knuckles, the tiger.
At the foot of the cliff, its mate. Two mice,
One black, one white, began to gnaw the root.

And by the traveller's head grew one
Juicy strawberry, so . . . hugging the root
The man reached out and plucked the fruit.

How sweet it tasted!

Christopher Logue

The Golden Road to Samarkand

HASSAN

> Sweet to ride forth at evening from the wells,
>   When shadows pass gigantic on the sand,
> And softly through the silence beat the bells
>   Along the Golden Road to Samarkand.

ISHAK

> We travel not for trafficking alone;
> By hotter winds our fiery hearts are fanned:
> For lust of knowing what should not be known
> We take the Golden Road to Samarkand.

MASTER OF THE CARAVAN

> Open the gate, O watchman of the night!

THE WATCHMAN

> Ho, travellers, I open. For what land
> Leave you the dim-moon city of delight?

MERCHANTS (*with a shout*)

> We take the Golden Road to Samarkand!
> (*The Caravan passes through the gate*)

THE WATCHMAN (*consoling the women*)

> What would ye, ladies? It was ever thus.
> Men are unwise and curiously planned.

A WOMAN

> They have their dreams, and do not think of us.

VOICES OF THE CARAVAN (*in the distance singing*)

> We take the Golden Road to Samarkand.

James Elroy Flecker

Fantasy in a Forest

(. . . 'And it is well known that the Unicorn by touching
the water with his Horn, doth render it free from Poison;
and the Creatures of the wild putteth their trust in him,
and do Drink thereof.' – *Beastiary* of Amelius of Gault.)

Between two unknown trees I stood
Within an Abyssinian wood.
Unseen beside a cold pool's brink,
I saw the beasts come down to drink, –
The elephant, the shy gazelle,
The leopard in his painted fell,[1]
The camel coloured like the sand,
The serpent like a burning brand,
The horse, giraffe, the red baboon
Down from the Mountains of the Moon,
The zebra striped with light and shade
Beside the lion, unafraid.

Around the pool they took their stand;
I could have touched them with my hand!
No creature moved, no creature leapt,
But all a curious silence kept,
And nothing in the forest stirred;
They waited as if for a word.

Then stepping lonely from the wild
He came, the white, the undefiled,
With ivory hoof and pearly horn, –
The one immaculate Unicorn!

Moving serenely to the pond,
Bending no blade nor ferny frond
Beneath the quiet of his tread;
He dipped his proud and lovely head,
And that dark fountain's veil was torn
By the sharp splendour of his horn.

Around the circle went a sigh
As if a breeze were passing by;
And then beside the curving brink
I saw the creatures crouch to drink
Those waters cleansed and strangely blest
By that unhuman exorcist.
They drank together, shy gazelle,
The leopard in his painted fell . . .

I saw these things the day I stood
Lost in that Abyssinian wood.

Leah Bodine Drake

1. pelt, skin

A Night with a Wolf

High up on the lonely mountains,
    Where the wild men watched and waited;
Wolves in the forest, and bears in the bush,
    And I on my path belated.

The rain and the night together
    Came down, and the wind came after,
Bending the props of the pine-tree roof,
    And snapping many a rafter.

I crept along in the darkness,
    Stunned, and bruised, and blinded;
Crept to a fir with thick-set boughs,
    And a sheltering rock behind it.

There, from the blowing and raining,
    Crouching, I sought to hide me.
Something rustled; two green eyes shone;
    And a wolf lay down beside me!

His wet fur pressed against me;
    Each of us warmed the other;
Each of us felt, in the stormy dark,
    That beast and man were brother.

And when the falling forest
    No longer crashed in warning,
Each of us went from our hiding place
    Forth in the wild, wet morning.

Bayard Taylor

The Boy

I'd like, above all, to be one of those
who drive with wild black horses through the night,
torches like hair uplifted in affright
when the great wind of their wild hunting blows.
I'd like to stand in front as in a boat,
tall, like a long floating flag unrolled.
And dark, but with a helmet made of gold,
restlessly flashing. And behind to ride
ten other looming figures side by side,
with helmets all unstable like my own,
now clear like glass, now old and blank like stone.
And one to stand by me and blow us space
with the brass trumpet that can blaze and blare,
blowing a black solitude through which we tear
like dreams that speed too fast to leave a trace.
Houses behind us fall upon their knees,
alleys cringe crookedly before our train,
squares break in flight: we summon and we seize:
we ride, and our great horses rush like rain.

Rainer Maria Rilke
translated from the German by
J. B. Leishman

Middle Ages

I heard a clash, and a cry,
And a horseman fleeing the wood.
The moon hid in a cloud.
Deep in shadow I stood.
  'Ugly work!' thought I,
Holding my breath.
    'Men must be cruel and proud,
    Jousting for death.'

With gusty glimmering shone
The moon; and the wind blew colder.
A man went over the hill,
Bent to his horse's shoulder.
  'Time for me to be gone.' . . .
Darkly I fled.
Owls in the wood were shrill,
And the moon sank red.

              Siegfried Sassoon

Eldorado

Gaily bedight,[1]
A gallant knight,
In sunshine and in shadow,
Had journeyed long,
Singing a song,
In search of Eldorado.

But he grew old –
This knight so bold –
And o'er his heart a shadow
Fell as he found
No spot of ground
That looked like Eldorado.

And, as his strength
Failed him at length,
He met a pilgrim shadow:
'Shadow,' said he,
'Where can it be,
This land of Eldorado?'

'Over the mountains
Of the Moon,
Down the valley of the Shadow,
Ride, boldly ride,'
The shade replied,
'If you seek for Eldorado.'

Edgar Allan Poe

1. equipped

Advice to a Knight

Wear modest armour; and walk quietly
In woods, where any noise is treacherous.
Avoid dragons and deceptive maidens.

Be polite to other men in armour,
Especially the fierce ones, who are often strong.
Treat all old men as they might be magicians.

So you may come back from your wanderings,
Clink proud and stiff into the queen's court
To doff your helmet and expect her thanks.

The young queen is amused at your white hair,
Asks you to show your notched and rusty sword,
And orders extra straw for your bedding.

Tomorrow put on your oldest clothes,
Take a stout stick and set off again,
It's safer that way if no more rewarding.

T. H. Jones

Action Man

Polar explorer
Action Man
Covers his ears with fur
In his bright red hood
And puts his ski-ing boots on.
As he bends his knees
And crouches over his skis
It begins to freeze,
Snowy mountains rise
Into frosty skies
And over the snow
He swoops towards the Pole.

Action Man puts on jump-boots
And parachute.
As he fastens his helmet
Under his chin
Clouds gather round
Looking like the ceiling
Of the roof of the world
Where they live
To people below –
And, pulling the ripcord,
Through the ceiling
The Red Devil dives.

Action Man puts on his silver suit
And heavily weighted boots.
As he puts his head
Inside his helmet
The countdown has started;
There is his rocket
Pointed like a pencil,
Ready to dot
A landing spot
On the moon.
Beneath it the fuel flares
And like an extra star
It shoots through the air.

The winds give a lion-like roar
And huge waves somersault
Like elephants onto the shore
As eagle-eyed Action Man
Puts his equipment on
And with his crew
Speeds to the rescue
In a motor boat
Or lowers a rope
From a twirling, whirling
Helicopter
While savage waves beneath
Snap their hungry teeth
But nothing can
Frighten Action Man.

Stanley Cook

Glorious it is

Glorious it is to see
The caribou flocking down from the forests
And beginning
Their wanderings to the north.
Timidly they watch
For the pitfalls of man.
Glorious it is to see
The great herds from the forests
Spreading out over plains of white.

Glorious it is to see
Early summer's short-haired caribou
Beginning to wander.
Glorious to see them trot
To and fro
Across the promontories,
Seeking for a crossing place.

Glorious it is
To see great musk oxen
Gathering in herds.
The little dogs they watch for
When they gather in herds.
Glorious to see.

Glorious it is
To see the long-haired winter caribou
Returning to the forests.
Fearfully they watch
For the little people,
While the herd follows the ebb-mark of the sea
With a storm of clattering hooves.
Glorious it is
When wandering time is come.

Unknown
translated from the Eskimo by
Dr Edmund Carpenter

The Works of the Lord
from Psalm 107

They that go down to the sea in ships,
That do business in great waters,
These see the works of the LORD
And his wonders in the deep.
For he commandeth, and raiseth the stormy wind,
Which lifteth up the waves thereof.
They mount up to the heaven, they go down again to the
    depth;
Their soul melteth away because of trouble.
They reel to and fro, and stagger like a drunken man,
And are at their wits' end.
Then they cry unto the LORD in their trouble,
And he bringeth them out of their distresses.
He maketh the storm a calm,
So that the waves thereof are still.

The Bible

A Wet Sheet and a Flowing Sea

A wet sheet and a flowing sea,
   A wind that follows fast
And fills the white and rustling sail
   And bends the gallant mast;
And bends the gallant mast, my boys,
   While like the eagle free
Away the good ship flies and leaves
   Old England on the lee.

O for a soft and gentle wind!
   I heard a fair one cry;
But give to me the snoring breeze
   And white waves heaving high;
And white waves heaving high, my lads,
   The good ship tight and free –
The world of waters is our home,
   And merry men are we.

There's tempest in yon hornèd moon,
   And lightning in yon cloud;
But hark the music, mariners!
   The wind is piping loud;
The wind is piping loud, my boys,
   The lightning flashes free –
While the hollow oak our palace is,
   Our heritage the sea.

Alan Cunningham

The Gallant Ship

Upon the gale she stooped her side,
And bounded o'er the swelling tide,
   As she were dancing home;
The merry seamen laughed to see
Their gallant ship so lustily
   Furrow the sea-green foam.

        Sir Walter Scott

from *The Rime of the Ancient Mariner*

With sloping masts and dipping prow,
As who pursued with yell and blow,
Still treads the shadow of his foe,
And forward bends his head,
The ship drove fast, loud roared the blast,
And southward aye we fled.

And now there came both mist and snow,
And it grew wondrous cold:
And ice, mast-high, came floating by,
As green as emerald.

And through the drifts the snowy clifts
Did send a dismal sheen:
Nor shapes of men nor beasts we ken –
The ice was all between.

The ice was here, the ice was there,
The ice was all around:
It cracked and growled, and roared and howled,
Like noises in a swound!

Samuel Taylor Coleridge

The Moon is Up

The moon is up: the stars are bright:
  The wind is fresh and free!
We're out to seek for gold tonight
  Across the silver sea!
The world is growing grey and old:
  Break out the sails again!
We're out to seek a Realm of Gold
  Beyond the Spanish Main.

We're sick of all the cringing knees,
  The courtly smiles and lies!
God, let thy singing Channel breeze
  Lighten our hearts and eyes!

Let love no more be bought and sold
  For earthly loss or gain;
We're out to seek an Age of Gold
  Beyond the Spanish Main.

Beyond the light of far Cathay,
  Beyond all mortal dreams,
Beyond the reach of night and day
  Our El Dorado gleams,
Revealing – as the skies unfold –
  A star without a stain,
The Glory of the Gates of Gold
  Beyond the Spanish Main.

     Alfred Noyes

Night in the Pacific
from *The Ballad of Kon-Tiki*

What words
Can paint the night,
When the sea was no darkness but a universe of light?
Lo, in their wake a shoal
Of little shrimps, all shining,
A sprinkle of red coal!
Drawn by the gleaming cabin lamp, the octopus,
The giant squid with green ghostly eyes,
Hugged and hypnotized;
While, fathoms below, in the pitch-black deep were
    gliding
Balloons of flashing fire, silver
Streaming meteors. O world of wonder!
O splendid pageantry!
Hour after dreamy hour they gazed spell-bound,
Trailing their fingers in the starry sea.

Ian Serraillier

Trade Winds

In the harbour, in the island, in the Spanish Seas,
Are the tiny white houses and the orange-trees,
And day-long, night-long, the cool and pleasant breeze
  Of the steady Trade Winds blowing.

There is the red wine, the nutty Spanish ale,
The shuffle of the dancers, the old salt's tale,
The squeaking fiddle, and the soughing in the sail
  Of the Steady Trade Winds blowing.

And o' nights there's fire-flies and the yellow moon,
And in the ghostly palm-trees the sleepy tune
Of the quiet voice calling me, the long low croon
  Of the steady Trade Winds blowing.

John Masefield

There was an Indian

There was an Indian, who had known no change
　　Who strayed content along a sunlit beach
Gathering shells. He heard a sudden strange
　　Commingled noise; looked up; and gasped for speech.
For in the bay, where nothing was before,
　　Moved on the sea, by magic, huge canoes,
With bellying cloth on poles, and not one oar,
　　And fluttering coloured signs and clambering crews.

And he, in fear, this naked man alone,
　　His fallen hands forgetting all their shells,
His lips gone pale, knelt low behind a stone,
　　And stared, and saw, and did not understand.
Columbus's doom-burdened caravels
　　Slant to the shore, and all their seamen land.

J. C. Squire

The Road

The moon sails o'er Long Mountain, and lights a
    sandstrip lone,
Where surf swims, silver shimmering, and shoreward
    breakers drone:
Along the forlorn stretches the night winds sweep and
    moan:
A shadow moves, slow creeping, athwart the whiteness
    thrown:
It speeds, it stops, and peers: a lance uplifts and stabs:
An Indian, silent, naked, hunting and spearing crabs.

A brigantine rides dipping, beneath the tropic moon,
With Spanish loot full laden, mantilla and doubloon,
For Morgan makes Port Royal, and bottles clink and
    clash,
And sailormen are cheering to see the shore-lights flash,
Carina, dark eyes glittering, bedecked with jingling rings,
Flutters to greet a gallant lad who many a moidore
    brings.

The self-same moon is lamping that gleaming arm
    to-night
Fanned by Caribbean breezes and curved for heart's
    delight,
But with the salt wind's sighing the sounds of laughter
    come
From dance-hall and from night-club, and motors throb
    and hum.
For man has built a roadway, a thoroughfare, you know,
Where Indian chevied scuttling crab a mort of years ago.

Reginald M. Murray

The Ship

There was no song nor shout of joy
   Nor beam of moon or sun,
When she came back from the voyage
   Long ago begun;
But twilight on the waters
   Was quiet and grey,
And she glided steady, steady and pensive,
   Over the open bay.

Her sails were brown and ragged,
   And her crew hollow-eyed,
But their silent lips spoke content
   And their shoulders pride;
Though she had no captives on her deck,
   And in her hold
There were no heaps of corn or timber
   Or silks or gold.

J. C. Squire

Westward! Westward!
from *The Song of Hiawatha*

On the shore stood Hiawatha,
Turned and waved his hand at parting;
On the clear and luminous water
Launched his birch-canoe for sailing,
From the pebbles of the margin
Shoved it forth into the water;
Whispered to it, 'Westward! westward!'
And with speed it darted forward.

And the evening sun descending
Set the clouds on fire with redness,
Burned the broad sky, like a prairie,
Left upon the level water
One long track and trail of splendour,
Down whose stream, as down a river,
Westward, westward Hiawatha
Sailed into the fiery sunset,
Sailed into the purple vapours,
Sailed into the dusk of evening.

H. W. Longfellow

Journey's End

O Mistress Mine
from *Twelfth Night*

O mistress mine, where are you roaming?
O! stay and hear; your true love's coming,
   That can sing both high and low.
Trip no further, pretty sweeting;
Journeys end in lovers meeting,
   Every wise man's son doth know.

William Shakespeare

On the Ridgeway

Thinking of those who walked here long ago
On this greenway in summer and in snow
She said, 'This is the oldest road we tread,
The oldest in the world?' 'Yes, love,' I said.

Andrew Young

The Traveller

Old man, old man, sitting on the stile,
Your boots are worn, your clothes are torn,
   Tell us why you smile.

Children, children, what silly things you are!
My boots are worn and my clothes are torn
   Because I've walked so far.

Old man, old man, where have you walked from?
Your legs are bent, your breath is spent –
   Which way did you come?

Children, children, when you're old and lame,
When your legs are bent and your breath is spent
   You'll know the way I came.

Old man, old man, have you far to go
Without a friend to your journey's end,
   And why are you so slow?

Children, children, I do the best I may:
I meet a friend at my journey's end
   With whom you'll meet some day.

Old man, old man, sitting on the stile,
How do you know which way to go,
   And why is it you smile?

Children, children, butter should be spread,
Floors should be swept and promises kept –
   And you should be in bed!

Raymond Wilson

The Snow

In no way that I chose to go
Could I escape the falling snow.

I shut my eyes, wet with my fears:
The snow still whispered at my ears.

I stopped my ears in deaf disguise:
The snow still fell before my eyes.

Snow was my comrade, snow my fate,
In a country huge and desolate.

My footsteps made a shallow space,
And then the snow filled up the place,

And all the walking I had done
Was on a journey not begun.

I did not know the distance gone,
But resolutely travelled on.

While silently on every hand
Fell the sorrow of the land,

And no way that I chose to go
Could lead me from the grief of snow.

Clifford Dyment

Our Journey had Advanced

Our journey had advanced;
Our feet were almost come
To that odd fork in Being's road,
Eternity by term.

Our pace took sudden awe,
Our feet reluctant led.
Before were cities, but between,
The forest of the dead.

Retreat was out of hope, –
Behind, a sealed route,
Eternity's white flag before,
And God at every gate.

Emily Dickinson

Echo

Thick is the darkness –
  Sunward, O sunward!
Rough is the highway –
  Onward, still onward!

Dawn harbours surely
  East of the shadows.
Facing us somewhere
  Spread the sweet meadows.

Upward and forward!
  Time will restore us:
Light is above us,
  Rest is before us.

W. E. Henley

Up-hill

Does the road wind up-hill all the way?
   Yes, to the very end.
Will the day's journey take the whole long day?
   From morn to night, my friend.

But is there for the night a resting-place?
   A roof for when the slow dark hours begin.
May not the darkness hide it from my face?
   You cannot miss that inn.

Shall I meet other wayfarers at night?
   Those who have gone before.
Then must I knock, or call when just in sight?
   They will not keep you standing at that door.

Shall I find comfort, travel-sore and weak?
   Of labour you shall find the sum.
Will there be beds for me and all who seek?
   Yea, beds for all who come.

Christina Rossetti

Requiem

Under the wide and starry sky,
   Dig the grave and let me lie.
Glad did I live and gladly die,
   And I laid me down with a will.

This be the verse you grave for me:
Here he lies where he longed to be;
Home is the sailor, home from sea,
   And the hunter home from the hill.

Robert Louis Stevenson

Index and
Acknowledgements

Index of First Lines

Index of Authors

Acknowledgements

The editor and publishers gratefully acknowledge permission to reproduce copyright poems in this book:

'Around Sheepwash' by Fleur Adcock, reprinted by permission of the author; extract from 'The End of the Road' by Hilaire Belloc from *Collected Poems*, reprinted by permission of A. D. Peters & Co. Ltd; 'The Fun Fair' by Isabel Best from *For Today and Tomorrow*, reprinted by permission of Unwin Hyman Ltd; 'The Midnight Skaters' by Edmund Blunden from *Poems of Many Years*, reprinted by permission of A. D. Peters & Co. Ltd; 'Changing the Wheel' by Bertolt Brecht, translated by Michael Hamburger, from *Poems 1913–1956* by Bertolt Brecht, reprinted by permission of Methuen, London; 'A Vagabond Song' by Bliss Carman, reprinted by permission of McClelland & Stewart; 'Glorious it is' translated by Dr Edmund Carpenter from *Anerca*, reprinted by permission of J. M. Dent & Sons (Canada) Ltd; 'The Dead Swagman' by Nancy Cato, reprinted from *The Dancing Bough* by permission of Angus & Robertson (Australia); 'The Little Cart' by Ch'ên Tsǔ-Lung, translated by Arthur Waley, reprinted from *170 Chinese Poems* by permission of Allen & Unwin; 'Floating on the Jo Yeh Stream in Spring' by Chi Wu-Ch'ien, translated by Soames Jenyns from *A Further Selection from the 300 Poems of the T'ang Dynasty*, reprinted by permission of John Murray (Publishers) Ltd; 'An Old Woman of the Road' by Padraic Colum from *The Poet's Circuits* (Oxford University Press, 1960), copyright holder could not be traced; 'Action Man' by Stanley Cook, reprinted by permission of the author; extract from 'The Seafarer', translated by Kevin Crossley-Holland, copyright holder of this translation; 'Gypsy Dance' by Linda Davies, reprinted by permission of Macmillan, London and Basingstoke; 'Dusk' by Walter Davies (Gwallter Mechain), translation reprinted by permission of Aran John; 'A Great Time' by W. H. Davies from *The Complete Poems of W. H. Davies*, reprinted by permission of the Executors of the W. H. Davies Estate and of Jonathan Cape Ltd; 'Minstrel' by Michael Dransfield from *Streets of the Long Voyage*, 1970, published by University of Queensland Press; 'Wanderlust' by Elizabeth Du Preez, reprinted by permission of J. J. Du Preez; 'The Snow' by Clifford Dyment, from *Poems 1935– 48* by Clifford Dyment reprinted by permission of J. M. Dent & Sons Ltd; 'The Road Not Taken' by Robert Frost from *The Poetry of Robert Frost*, edited by Edward Connery Latham, reprinted by permission of the Estate of Robert Frost and of Jonathan Cape Ltd, copyright 1916 © 1969 by Holt, Rinehart and Winston. Copyright 1944 by Robert Frost. Reprinted by permission of Henry Holt and Company, Inc; 'The Legs' by Robert Graves from *Collected Poems*, reprinted by permission of A. P. Watt Ltd on behalf of the Executors of the Estate of Robert Graves; 'Tramp' by Gregory Harrison, reprinted by permission of the author; 'Boy With Kite' by Phoebe Hesketh, reprinted by permission of the author; 'The Gipsy Girl' by Ralph Hodgson, reprinted by permission of Macmillan, London and Basingstoke; 'The Harvest Moon' by Ted Hughes from *Seasons Songs*, reprinted by permission of Faber and Faber Ltd; 'Summer Night' by James Kirkup from *The Prodigal Son*, reprinted by permission of the author; 'Poetry of Departure' by Philip Larkin, reprinted from *The Less Deceived* by permission of the Marvell Press; 'Clearing at Dawn' by Li Po, translated by Arthur Waley, reprinted from *Chinese Poems* by permission of Allen and Unwin; 'Good Taste' by Christopher Logue, reprinted by permission of the author;

189

Basingstoke; 'Plucking the Rushes' translated by Arthur Waley, reprinted from *101 Chinese Poems* by permission of Allen & Unwin; 'High on the Hill' by Tom Wright, reprinted by permission of the author: 'The Lake Isle of Innisfree', 'The Fiddler of Dooney and 'To a Squirrel at Kyle-na-no' by W. B. Yeats from *The Collected Poems of W. B. Yeats*, reprinted by permission of A. P. Watt Ltd on behalf of Michael B. Yeats and Macmillan, London Ltd; 'Wiltshire Downs', 'A Child's Voice' and 'On the Ridgeway' by Andrew Young from *The Poetical Works* by Andrew Young, reprinted by permission of Martin Secker and Warburg Ltd.

Every effort has been made to trace copyright holders, but in a few cases this has proved impossible. The editor and publishers would like to hear from any copyright holders not acknowledged.